# THE SKULL IN THE ROCK

# THE SKULL IN THE ROCK

## HOW A SCIENTIST, A BOY, AND GOOGLE EARTH OPENED A NEW WINDOW ON HUMAN ORIGINS

By Lee R. Berger and Marc Aronson

NATIONAL GEOGRAPHIC

WASHINGTON, D.C.

To Jackie, Megan, and Matthew, who have not only supported my desire to explore our past, but who join me in the adventure.—L.B.

To my family for joining me in this adventure, and putting up with the stress of the dash to the finish line.—M.A.

Copyright © 2012 Lee R. Berger and Aronson & Glenn LLC
All rights reserved. Reproduction of the whole or any part of the contents without written permission from the publisher is prohibited.

**A Book by Aronson & Glenn LLC**
**Produced by** Marc Aronson and John W. Glenn
**Book design, decorative illustrations, and production by** Jon Glick, mouse+tiger •
**Copyediting by** Sharon Brinkman • **Additional research by** Susan Bartle

**Published by the National Geographic Society**
John M. Fahey, Jr., *Chairman of the Board and Chief Executive Officer*
Timothy T. Kelly, *President*
Declan Moore, *Executive Vice President; President, Publishing and Digital Media*
Melina Gerosa Bellows, *Executive Vice President; Chief Creative Officer,*
    *Books, Kids, and Family*

**Prepared by the Book Division**
Hector Sierra, *Senior Vice President and General Manager*
Nancy Laties Feresten, *Senior Vice President, Editor in Chief, Children's Books*
Jonathan Halling, *Design Director, Books and Children's Publishing*
Jay Sumner, *Director of Photography, Children's Publishing*
Jennifer Emmett, *Editorial Director, Children's Books*
Eva Absher-Schantz, *Managing Art Director, Children's Publishing*
Carl Mehler, *Director of Maps*
R. Gary Colbert, *Production Director*
Jennifer A. Thornton, *Director of Managing Editorial*

**Staff for This Book**
Jennifer Emmett, *Project Editor*
James Hiscott, Jr., *Art Director*
Lori Epstein, *Senior Illustrations Editor*
Kate Olesin, *Assistant Editor*
Kathryn Robbins, *Design Production Assistant*
Hillary Moloney, *Illustrations Assistant*
Carl Mehler, *Director of Maps*
Grace Hill, *Associate Managing Editor*
Joan Gossett, *Production Editor*
Lewis R. Bassford, *Production Manager*
Susan Borke, *Legal and Business Affairs*

**Manufacturing and Quality Management**
Phillip L. Schlosser, *Senior Vice President*
Chris Brown, *Vice President*
George Bounelis, *Vice President, Production Services*
Nicole Elliott, *Manager*
Rachel Faulise, *Manager*
Robert L. Barr, *Manager*

PRECEDING PAGE: A grassy plain unfolds just above the eroded cave of Malapa, discovery site of *Australopithecus sediba*.

The National Geographic Society is one of the world's largest nonprofit scientific and educational organizations. Founded in 1888 to "increase and diffuse geographic knowledge," the Society's mission is to inspire people to care about the planet. It reaches more than 400 million people worldwide each month through its official journal, *National Geographic*, and other magazines; National Geographic Channel; television documentaries; music; radio; films; books; DVDs; maps; exhibitions; live events; school publishing programs; interactive media; and merchandise. National Geographic has funded more than 10,000 scientific research, conservation and exploration projects and supports an education program promoting geographic literacy. For more information, visit www.nationalgeographic.com.

For more information, please call 1-800-NGS LINE (647-5463) or write to the following address:
National Geographic Society
1145 17th Street N.W.
Washington, D.C. 20036-4688 U.S.A.

Visit us online at nationalgeographic.com/books

For librarians and teachers: ngchildrensbooks.org

More for kids from National Geographic: kids.nationalgeographic.com

For information about special discounts for bulk purchases, please contact National Geographic Books Special Sales: ngspecsales@ngs.org

For rights or permissions inquiries, please contact National Geographic Books Subsidiary Rights: ngbookrights@ngs.org

Aronson, Marc.
 The skull in the rock : how a scientist, a boy, and Google Earth opened a new window on human origins / by Marc Aronson and Lee Berger.
  p. cm.
Includes bibliographical references and index.
ISBN 978-1-4263-1010-2 (hardcover : alk. paper) -- ISBN 978-1-4263-1053-9 (library binding : alk. paper)
 1. Fossil hominids--South Africa--Witwatersrand Region. 2. Human beings--Origin. 3. Human evolution--South Africa--Witwatersrand Region. 4. Excavations (Archaeology)--South Africa--Witwatersrand Region. 5. Paleoanthropology. 6. Berger, Lee R. I. Berger, Lee R. II. Title.
GN282.A695 2012
569.9096822--dc23

                              2012012943

Printed in China
12/TS/2

# CONTENTS

## CHAPTER ONE

# THE **FIRST** BONE

## "Dad, I've found a fossil."

Nine-year-old Matthew Berger was fossil hunting with his dad when he stumbled and spied a brown rock with a thin yellow bone stuck in it. Matthew was lucky: His father is Professor Lee Berger, a scientist who has devoted his life to finding the remains of our ancient ancestors. They had often gone exploring together in the brown limestone hills and scraggly trees just outside of Johannesburg, South Africa. So many important fossils have been found in this area that it is called the Cradle of Humankind and is protected by the government and listed as a World Heritage Site.

Though only half an hour from one of the largest cities in Africa, the Cradle belongs to animals—visitors are watched by troops of baboons, dodged by scampering warthogs, measured by soaring eagles. The Bergers always bring their Rhodesian ridgebacks with them in their customized Jeep—since leopards and other predators prowl nearby, and the dogs smell and sense them in time to give warning. On this pleasant August morning in 2008, Matthew called out to his dad—and opened a door two million years back in time.

Some day, Matthew's words may be famous, the way we honor "What hath God wrought?" the first telegraph message sent in 1844, or "Mr. Watson, come here" the first telephone call 32 years later. What he found was that important. But that is not what his dad first thought. Every other time they had gone out together, Matthew

Because he was trained to look for fossils, Matthew spotted the fossil that was just barely sticking out of this rock (OPPOSITE).

found the remains of ancient antelopes—fossils that are quite common in the area. As Dr. Berger came closer, Matthew could tell that his dad assumed it was just another old antelope and was trying to be nice by pretending to be interested. That is exactly what Dr. Berger was thinking until he was about fifteen feet (4.6 m) from his son, and could focus.

Right then, just at that precise moment, he froze. His world went black and white. Time stopped. Matthew was holding a gift from the past so precious almost nothing like it had ever been found. And the one person in the world who knew that for sure was Dr. Lee Berger. For the fossil was a clavicle, the thin connecting bone across the shoulder that humans and our ancestors share—and that athletes in contact sports sometimes break. The bone is so fragile, not one of the famous skeletons of prehumans still has a complete one. Yet when he was a graduate student, Dr. Berger had written his Ph.D. thesis on just that bone and three others that would become important in this story, the bones that make up the upper arm.

Lee's snapshot taken on site as Matthew points to the clavicle

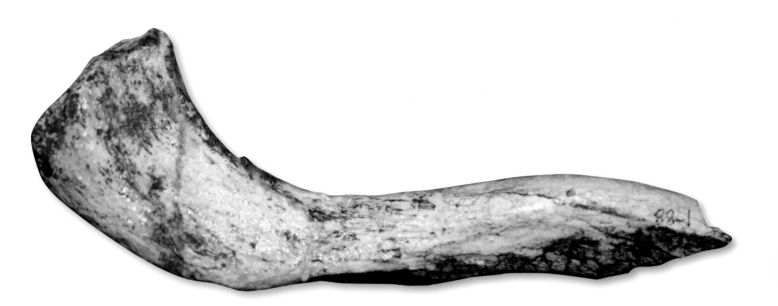

The clavicle itself, removed from the stone. It is approximately 2.75 inches (7 cm) long. This is the first clue that opened a new door to the story of human evolution.

Because Matthew had trained his eyes, he recognized a fossil. Because his father had studied that part of the body, he realized the treasure in his son's hands. For Dr. Berger, it would have been enough to find that one special bone. But the clavicle was just the beginning. It was the rabbit hole beckoning Alice, the wardrobe flung open to Narnia, the first clue to what is becoming an entirely new way of understanding human evolution.

It is easy to envy the Bergers, to wish you or I had the chance to find the bone, which turned out to be part of a nearly complete skeleton of an entirely new species (*Australopithecus sediba*) previously unknown to science. But as Dr. Berger says, that is getting it totally wrong. Because the most important thing about the find is the doors it opens for the next new discovery. Every door leads somewhere, even those that seem closed—that is what Dr. Berger's own life story told him.

# HOW TO FIND A FOSSIL.

Finding a fossil is hard, but if you know what to look for, you can pick one out from all the other rocks and soil around it. Here Lee is at a potential fossil-bearing site in the Free State of South Africa. **1** First he looks for an area of erosion that might reveal rocks that are older than those on the surface. **2** Next he narrows his search to places where fossils might be eroding out of the surrounding soil. **3** Lee is looking for "oddities" or "anomalies," rocks or objects whose colors do not match the surrounding soil. In this case, he has spotted a white fleck. **4** When he gets closer, he can see that it is part of the lower jaw, or mandible, of an ancient antelope. **5** Notice the shiny enamel of the teeth and the paler look of the bone. The mandible Lee found in this hunt is more than 100,000 years old.

2 ▼

3 ▼    4 ▶

5 ▶

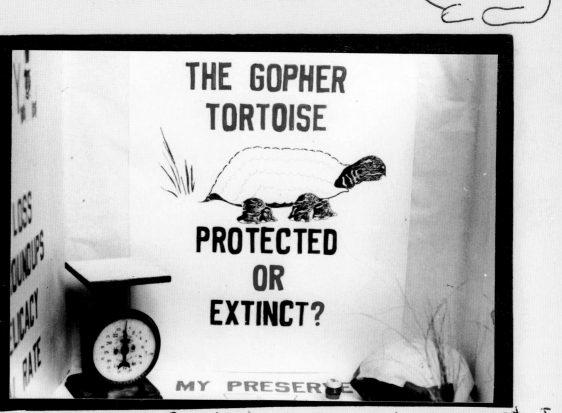

THE GOPHER
TORTOISE

PROTECTED
OR
EXTINCT?

MY PRESERVE

My Gopher Project is my pet project. I have
started a preserve and this is one of
my many exhibits and demonstrations gi...

MEMBERS OF THE LAND JUDGING TEAM, shown above, are left to
right, Michael Hayes, Rod Berger, Pam Skinner, Danny Smith, James
Williams, Craig Howard, and Chris Miccoli.

I started the land    team in 1980
and we improved this year - 5th at
District. I was 3rd high on team

# CHAPTER TWO
# SEEING THE ANOMALY

**If you were looking** for young Lee Rogers Berger back when he was growing up in the town of Sylvania, in Screven County, Georgia, you would have needed strong lungs. When he didn't absolutely need to be inside the house, or at school, he was sure to be outdoors. That is the kind of boy he was—no shoes all summer long until he was old enough to follow the seasons through fishing, hunting, and generally just waiting to see what adventure nature would bring. If a farmer was plowing his fields, there would be Lee scouring the furrows for arrowheads. Put a bow in his hands, and he'd keep practicing until he was state archery champion. Bumping along in the back of the family pickup (in the days when a ride in an open truck meant standing up and holding on, no seat belts), he had his eye out for strange or interesting or injured animals. All this time outside allowed him to collect his scouting merit badges at a good clip, earning his way up to Eagle Scout, and to join the 4H Club and Future Farmers of America.

The Bergers were not exactly farmers—his mom was a math professor, and his dad worked in an office. Although they did not have much money, Lee, his brother Lamont, and their parents often moved to Savannah, on the coast, in the summer, then back to rural Sylvania, like many Georgia families at the time. But they were not far from the land either. Lee's dad always wanted to be a geologist, which was one step away from Lee's grandfather—who had lost many of his fingers hunting for oil as a wildcatter in West

Lee at age seven (ABOVE). By the time he was a teenager, "Rod"—as he was known, after his middle name—was rounding up his friends to help protect the gopher tortoise (OPPOSITE).

*I have collections of Indian Artifacts, fish, stamps and cartoons.*

Whether it was arrowheads or bones, Lee collected the interesting anomalies he found in the fields near his home.

Texas. Wildcatters are the wiry, tough men who set out on their own, with whatever rig they can beg, borrow, or steal, to find oil—black gold.

One day, Lee's grandfather showed him a sealed chest. He flung open the lid, and there, inside, were thousands of pieces of paper—stock certificates from all of the oil companies he had been part of—each one a dream that had gone bust. Yet he was not bitter—wildcatters admire a man who has failed many times—it means he has tried and had the guts to go on.

Lee's dad decided to put his love of the land aside and provide for his family. But Lee inherited his grandfather's spirit—he loves a grand quest, an all-in roll of the dice. He is that restless boy who throws himself into his current interest until he masters it but then needs a new goal, a new passion, a new hill to climb. Those who don't know such boys call them easily distracted. Those who do, know they are hungry for adventure.

As Lee wandered the fields and pine forests of Screven County he practiced reading the land. It takes two skills to be a wildcatter: You have to know the terrain; and because you are so good at that, you train your eyes to notice what is different, what doesn't fit, what Lee calls "the anomaly." The first anomaly that made a difference to Rod (as Lee was then known) was an animal that spent most of its time underground.

Like its name suggests, the gopher tortoise likes to dig a snug home for itself underground. From his perch in the back of a truck, Lee started to notice a bad pattern—an anomaly: one, two, far too many dead and injured gopher tortoises. Why was that? And what could he do about it?

Some deadly snakes are happy that gopher tortoises carve out nice homes for them. But a human family is not eager to have their kids playing near snakes, and one quick way to avoid that is to send gasoline down any holes you see—and if some tortoises die along with the snakes, well that is one less hole-digger to worry about. Worse yet, when pine forests were harvested for timber, the burrows dug out by tortoises were destroyed.

Lee had to do something, but what? He convinced his parents to turn part of the land where they raised pigs and cows into a refuge for gopher tortoises. Now every jolting ride in the pickup was a potential rescue mission. Word spread of this new idea—a nature preserve founded by a teenager to save a local animal—and in 1984, Lee was named Georgia's Youth Conservationist of the Year. As the honoree, he got to speak to the state's representatives about the gopher tortoise. Today, while the animal is threatened, and it is still legal in Georgia to send gas down a burrow to clean out snakes, the gopher tortoise is the state reptile.

An adult gopher tortoise heading toward the burrow it has dug in the sandy soil.

Observe, notice, act, change the world: that is what Lee's childhood taught him. But how did he get from Georgia to South Africa, and from tortoises to fossils?

Through the covers of a book.

## CHAPTER THREE
# LUCY

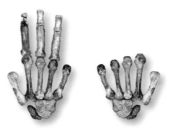

**On November 24, 1974,** at the end of a morning of fossil hunting in Ethiopia, a young paleoanthropologist named Donald Johanson followed a hunch to look in one more spot and saw first an arm bone, then a leg bone, then ribs. And then it hit him— there in the earth was nearly the entire skeleton of something, someone—which turned out to be Lucy, an ancestor from 3.2 million years ago. After carefully describing his find to the scientific world, Johanson told his personal story to the general public in a book simply called *Lucy. Lucy* changed Lee's life.

In his typical way, Lee had been on a roller coaster of ups and downs: he got into Vanderbilt, a fine university, on a Navy scholarship, then dropped out when he realized he was never going to be the lawyer or politician his parents imagined. He experimented with working in TV news and even became a national hero when he rescued a woman who was drowning. But his heart was not in chasing after police cars and filming local events. Back in college at Georgia Southern he began to picture himself as a dinosaur hunter, looking for the fossils of the next *T.-rex*. And then one afternoon at the library, he saw *Lucy*.

*Lucy* tells the story of how the author found "our oldest human ancestor... and who she was." From the first page on, Johanson, a serious, skilled paleoanthropologist, talks about "training your eye to see what you need to see," and being lucky. Training your

After Lucy was fully excavated, experts working with an artist created this plausible reconstruction (OPPOSITE) of what she might have looked like when she walked the Earth 3.2 million years ago.

Donald Johanson faces a composite *Australopithecus afarensis* skull (ABOVE). Lee as the alert young Naval recruit (RIGHT).

eye—that was exactly what Lee had learned from his grandfather and had been doing since childhood. And luck—now that was interesting—looking for the fossils of our ancestors is like hunting for oil, but thousands of times more difficult.

Lee estimates that the odds of finding the bones of our oldest ancestors are ten million to one—that is the kind of gamble he likes. As he says, "I always want to push boundaries." That is not just because he likes to take big risks—though he does —but because he wants to make big discoveries, and there is no larger challenge than helping to solve the mystery of human origins.

How, and why, did we evolve from apes? Which came first, walking on two legs or having a hand that made it easy to use tools? What about our brains—which are much larger than those of chimps and organized in different ways—how did that happen?

Reading *Lucy* gave Lee a vision of his life goal: hunting for the most crucial, and precious, clues to the story of humankind. But *Lucy* was also a warning: fossil hunting requires the perfect blend of knowledge, guts, and luck. Lee had found what he loved: the most difficult mystery of all.

**RIVER RESCUE:** In 1986, Lee was working as a news cameraman at TV station WTOC in Savannah, Georgia. At three in the morning on September 18, he heard on his police scanner a report that a woman had fallen into the Savannah River. He rushed to the scene, dove into the water, and rescued the drowning woman. Lee's bravery was honored many times, and WTOC filmed a special about their homegrown hero. The photos on this page are taken from that broadcast. As with the gopher tortoise, Lee saw, acted, and made a difference.

*November* 1986

## Savannah Police Department
SAVANNAH, GEORGIA

*Rod Bergen*

IN RECOGNITION OF YOUR OUTSTANDING BRAVERY AND CONCERN FOR THE LIFE OF A FELLOW HUMAN BEING. ON SEPTEMBER 18, 1986 YOU RISKED YOUR OWN LIFE TO DIVE INTO THE WATERS OF THE SAVANNAH RIVER TO HELP SAVE THE LIFE OF A DROWNING WOMAN. YOUR ACTIONS DEMONSTRATE YOUR DEEP CARING FOR OTHERS AND SUPPORT OF THE SAVANNAH POLICE DEPARTMENT. YOUR EFFORTS ARE THE REASON ... REFLECTS THE FACT THAT YOU ARE WILLING TO GO A... YOU ARE COMMENDED FOR AN OUT...

### The Honor Medal
FOR HEROIC ACTION AT THE RISK OF HIS OWN LIFE
IS AWARDED BY THE BOY SCOUTS OF AMERICA UPON THE
RECOMMENDATION OF THE NATIONAL COURT OF HONOR
ON March 10 19 87 TO
*Rod Berger*

On September 19, 1986, Eagle Scout, District Committeeman Rod Berger, 20, was on duty at 4:00 a.m. in the WTOC-TV news room when he heard a call on the police radio telling of a woman in trouble in the Savannah River. He responded to the call to film the rescue efforts for television. Once on the scene he saw that police rescue efforts were not working and the victim was being swept down river toward the sea. He put his camera down, jumped into the river, and swam to the victim. Fighting the swift current and struggling woman he brought her to safety. Rod Berger saved the woman and exemplified the Boy Scout motto, "Be Prepared."

## Cheers
To cameraman Rod Berger of station WTOC, Savannah, Ga. While taping the futile efforts of police to rescue a drowning woman in the Savannah River, Berger, 23, put down his camera gear, jumped into the water, swam 40 yards and pulled the woman back to the shore and safety.

*"You're an example for all of us..."*
Sen. Sam Nunn

## The TV Column
TUESDAY, SEPTEMBER 23

**State Digest**
TV photographer jumps into river to save a woman

**Missed the Story, But ...**

19

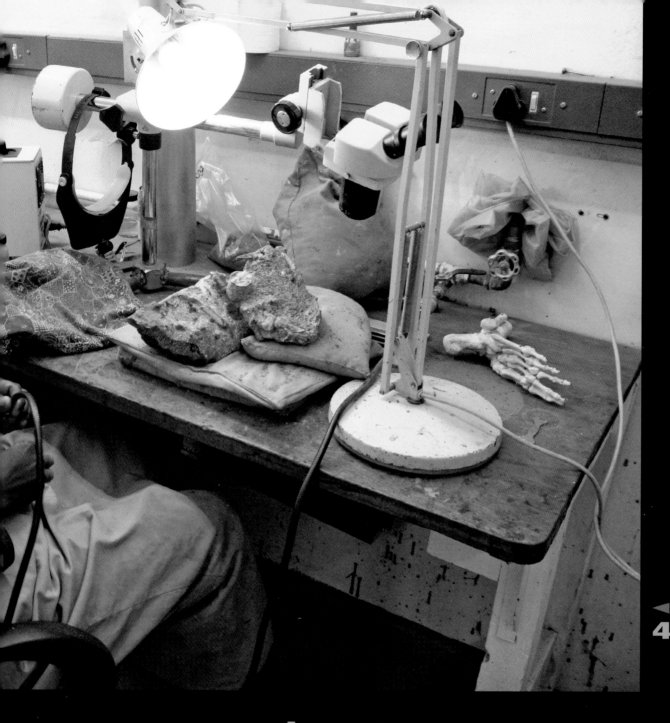

**FROM DIG TO LAB** **1** This scene from Malapa shows the beginning of the long process through which Lee and his team removed fossils from the ground and turned them into pieces of history you can actually hold in your hand. **2** Sometimes fossils are found in hard rock and have to be drilled out carefully using magnifying lenses and special drills. **3** When fossils are held in soft soil they can be removed by using water and a thin wire sieve. If the fossil is encased in rock when it arrives in the lab, a skilled worker carefully excavates the rock around the bone without touching it, using only a special drill and a microscope. **4** The painstaking work of excavating and cleaning fossils can take months. Modern technology can allow us to "digitally" prepare a fossil without ever touching it, using X-rays and computers. See Seeing Inside

## CHAPTER FOUR

# THE HUNTERS SET A TRAP

**Gladysvale Cave,** Cradle of Humankind, South Africa, 1994.

Lee was in his favorite spot—a cave he had been exploring
for years, even when he had to dodge prowling leopards—when he
glanced up at his audience. A troop of vervet monkeys was seated at
the edge of a cliff opposite the cave amusing itself by watching him.
Suddenly they were alert. Vervets have an alarm cry that they teach
their young—a sound so carefully passed on, some scientists believe it
is a primitive form of animal language. The monkeys began screaming:
Up there in the sky was danger, a black eagle. The monkeys rushed
away from its path … straight into the trap. The first eagle had been
a decoy, and the monkeys fell for it, for now a second eagle, the real
hunter, swooped down from the opposite direction and instantly
picked off an adult male.

Lee had never seen an eagle taking on an animal as large as a
monkey. He jumped up, rushed to his car, and sped off to the nearby
nest to see what would happen next. There lay scattered the bones
of the two hunters' many kills—some as large as a baboon. His mind
began spinning—right back to the reason he was in South Africa, and a
key discovery made there in 1924.

Back in the '20s, miners searching for limestone were still blasting
away in the area that is now the Cradle of Humankind. One day as
they worked in a mine outside of a place called Taung—the Place of

This painting
captures what it
might have been
like when the young
Taung Child looked
up into the sky as
a hunting crowned
eagle soared
overhead (OPPOSITE).

An African crowned eagle is a skilled predator that can weigh up to nine pounds (4 kg) and have a wingspan of seven feet (2 m).

the Lion—they noticed a pile of bones in the rubble, including a tiny skull. A miner was smart enough to put it into a box and send it to Dr. Raymond Dart—a scientist at the University of the Witwatersrand in Johannesburg. Dr. Dart figured out that the skull belonged to a child of about three years old. Then came the revelation: he saw that the opening for where the spine would have gone fit an animal that walked on two legs—not a chimp swinging from trees.

Dart announced that the Taung Child was the fossil of a previously unknown animal fitting between chimpanzees and humans. He named a new genus and species—*Australopithecus africanus*—the Southern Ape of Africa. That was the first human ancestor ever discovered in Africa. And while for decades experts in Europe refused to believe Dr. Dart, the Taung Child is now accepted as one of the most important fossils ever found. Indeed, after a terrifically lucky first day on a dig in Kenya where he found a hominin fossil, Lee had come to South Africa first to study and then to follow in Dr. Dart's footsteps, continuing the search that had begun with the Taung Child. But there was always a mystery about the skull and the bones found with it.

The Taung Child was found with many animal remains, most of them small, but no other hominins. Why? Dr. Dart believed that this was the home site of killer apes who left the bones of their victims. Later scholars assumed large cats had once lunched there. But the skeletons did not match the usual collection of leopard prey. Who killed the Taung Child?

As Lee's eyes ranged over the nest of the two eagle hunters, he recognized the skeletons—they were very similar to those found near the Taung Child. In fact the damage on the bones of the eagles' prey was the same as that on the fossils from Taung. Could an eagle have both killed and managed to fly off with a three-year-old australopithecine? Lee and his colleague Dr. Ron Clarke wrote a paper suggesting the idea. Many scientists were skeptical. They just could not picture one of our ancestors as the victim of a bird feeding its own young. The controversy over the eagle theory was hardly Lee's only problem. In fact, by 2000 it looked like his entire dream of following in Johanson's footsteps was doomed to failure.

In this staged shot, an eagle hovers ominously over the actual skull of the Taung Child.

# CHAPTER FIVE
# "WHAT IS RIGHT IN FRONT OF MY EYES THAT I AM MISSING?"

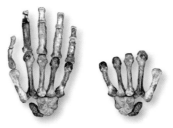

In 1994, Lee found his first hominin fragment at Gladysvale, carefully stored it in this box, and proudly displayed the find to the camera (OPPOSITE, TOP). Gladysvale (OPPOSITE, BOTTOM) yielded five more fragments, but by 2000 Lee was not sure what to do next.

**Lee first began** working in the Gladysvale Cave in 1991 and soon found teeth and other traces of ancient hominins. Terrific: this was the first early hominin site found in South Africa since 1948. Indeed, when he won the National Geographic Society's first Research and Exploration prize in 1997, Lee used his award money to carefully survey the region—looking for other possible fossil sites. But by the beginning of the new century, it seemed his luck was failing him.

As of 2000 Lee had only located a few fossil fragments—some more australopithecine teeth and bones to add to South Africa's chest of ancient treasures. And then an important scientist, one of the giants of the field, published an article arguing that there probably were no new fossil fields to be discovered and that the remaining sites were rapidly being exhausted. The field was dry and would only get drier.

It was hard to argue with the article, especially when Lee's own expensive survey failed to yield any important new discoveries. He was right back where he had been when he left Vanderbilt—as adrift and depressed as only a passionate explorer can be when he cannot find the next adventure. Lee's lifetime quest was over, since no one was going to sponsor him to go out in the field. The field was changing; computer technology for examining the remains already found seemed to be the future for the science. From now on, research into human origins would take place on screens and in gigabytes of digital memory. The door to the great outdoors appeared closed.

Restless, Lee looked for new challenges. He filmed a TV documentary series on exploration. Armed with his camera, he tramped through South Africa's great game parks and then wrote guidebooks for other visitors. He became a master diver, so that any vacation would give him a chance to range around the ocean floor. But even these efforts created some flack. A TV special built around discoveries he made diving on a Pacific island annoyed a small but vocal group of his scientific peers. And then, in 2005, Lee read an article.

The white arrows point to the signs of eagle pecks in the eye sockets of the Taung Child.

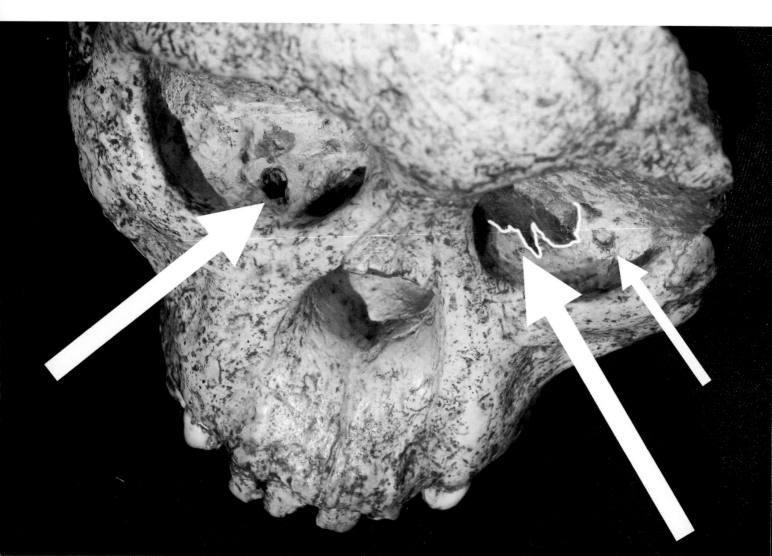

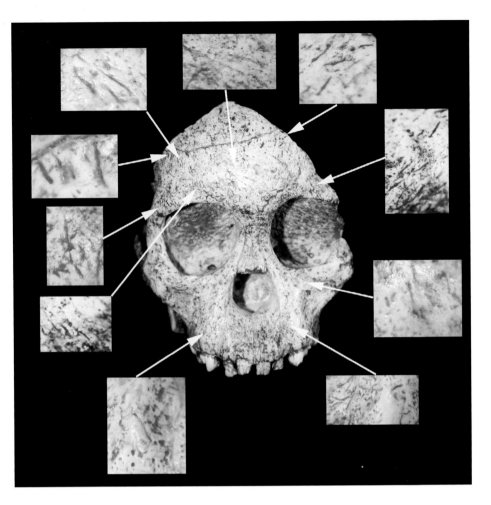

Careful searching of the Taung Child fossil showed potential eagle scratches all over the skull.

Ten years after Berger and Clarke proposed the eagle theory, scientists at Ohio State University set out to study African crowned eagles. They learned exactly how eagles hunted, how they flew off with their supper, and what the resulting collection of bones looked like in a nest. Every single skull held similar marks—notches cut by sharp talons and a probing beak into the eye sockets. Lee rushed to his office, opened the strong safe that guarded the Taung Child skull, and carefully examined the fossil. The exact same markings found in modern eagle kills were clearly visible inside the eye sockets of the tiny child. Proof. Case closed—and opened.

For 80 years scientists had looked at that very skull and not seen what was in front of their eyes. They had missed the anomaly. "What am I not seeing," Lee wondered. "What is right in front of my eyes that I am missing?"

Everything—as he would learn in the last days of December 2007.

## CHAPTER SIX
# IF YOU LOOK WITH NEW EYES YOU SEE NEW THINGS

**Lee is like so many of us**—when he turns on his computer or tablet, he is eager to try out whatever new programs and apps it offers. As 2007 came to a close, he noticed an option he had somehow missed: Google Earth. Of course he had to plug in his address and see his street, his home, his office at school. That was fun, what next?

For 17 years, Lee had explored the brown hills of the Cradle, following in the footsteps of one great scientist after another, back to Dr. Dart himself. There may not be a single area on this planet that has been as closely examined for possible hominin fossil sites. Could he look at the Cradle through Google Earth? You can't write in, "second scraggly tree from the left near where the antelope hides at midday" as a search question. But the survey Lee had commissioned with the National Geographic prize money meant he had GPS coordinates for the hills and valleys he knew so well. Here was Gladysvale Cave, where he had seen the eagles kill a monkey. There were the Sterkfontein Caves that had yielded Little Foot, the fossil hominin Dr. Clarke had been studying for more than a decade. So far so good. But what was this?

As Lee shifted from plugging in large features to smaller sites, what he was seeing on his screen did not look right. What

These screen captures (OPPOSITE) show the actual Google Earth images Lee viewed as he zoomed in from Africa as a whole to the region in the Cradle of Humankind he had been exploring for 17 years. The last image shows a cluster of trees in the Cradle marking the site of a cave (INDICATED BY ARROW). The search continues on the following pages.

should have been a hill, was a stream, what should have been one side of a cave, was another. The anomaly alarm bell started to ring in his mind.

Half of the problem was easy to solve: it turned out that the global satellite positioning that Google Earth used deliberately had small errors in it. The U.S. Defense Department that created the images matched to GPS coordinates did not want to hand potential enemies precise information they could use to launch missiles. Now Lee Berger, Eagle Scout, explorer, scientist, would have to come to his computer and slowly, carefully, figure out how much he had to adjust the image and the coordinates so that a cave appeared where it was supposed to be. He had to look, and look, and look again at the Cradle—but at a different angle, not from the ground, but from the eye in the sky.

This map highlights the areas where important hominin fossils have been found. The cluster including Malapa is in the heart of the Cradle of Humankind.

Google™

Looking down, oh so carefully examining the Google Earth image, he began to pick out features he had not noticed in 17 years. Looking with just their eyes, he and his colleagues had located some 130 caves and 20 potential fossil sites. But what was that cluster of trees hiding? Was that a trace of a seam, a fault line? If so, might there be caves along it he'd missed? Every new depression in the earth could be a collapsed cave—a place where fossil bones might be covered, caught, saved from harm. By the middle of 2008 he had located more than 600 caves and more than 30 new fossil sites. He and generations of previous scientists had been blind—seeing only what they expected to see. Hidden in the dips and folds of the Cradle were possibilities beyond imagining. Now all he had to do was to go out and explore them.

In this view, Gladysvale is over the hill to the left. In the last week of July 2008, Lee explored the cave beneath the stand of trees in the foreground **1** and also the cave indicated by the star **2**. Lee then traveled to the saddle of hills immediately behind, and there, down the slope behind the right hill, he came across Malapa **3**.

Lee striding and Tau scampering at his heels on the way to Malapa

Where to start? Since Lee was looking for new sites, he thought he had better begin in a new spot. So he went out in the field as far from Gladysvale and other familiar places as he could go. One more mistake—which he calls "backyard syndrome." You don't expect to find anything new in a place you know very well. But why not? The very fact that it is so familiar may mean you hardly notice it at all. You see what you remember and expect to see.

Slowly, Lee moved back, closer and closer to home ground. He loaded his dog Tau into the Jeep, sometimes brought Matthew or his teenaged daughter Megan along, or even a friend to keep him company, and went hunting. May turned to June, June to July, July ebbed away. On screen he noticed a cluster of trees in a place he later decided to call Malapa ("homestead," in Sesotho, a local language), a short hop from Gladysvale. Trees in clumps are often a sign of a collapsed cave, but he had explored this area back in 1998 and was sure it held no secrets. But then, on August 1 he noticed a track in the ground—a sign that miners had blasted in the area looking for limestone. Walking along that track Lee found evidence of 47 previously unknown caves. He returned two weeks later with Tau, Job Kibii, a postdoctoral student from his lab, and a guest.

And it was there, walking just outside the circle of trees, that Matthew stumbled and called out,

"Dad, I've found a fossil."

On August 1, 2008, after seeing a cluster of what looked like caves while viewing Google Earth **1** (stars at top), Lee discovered Malapa **2** (star at bottom). Two weeks later, on August 15, Lee returned to Malapa with Matthew, and Matthew found the first important part of sediba.

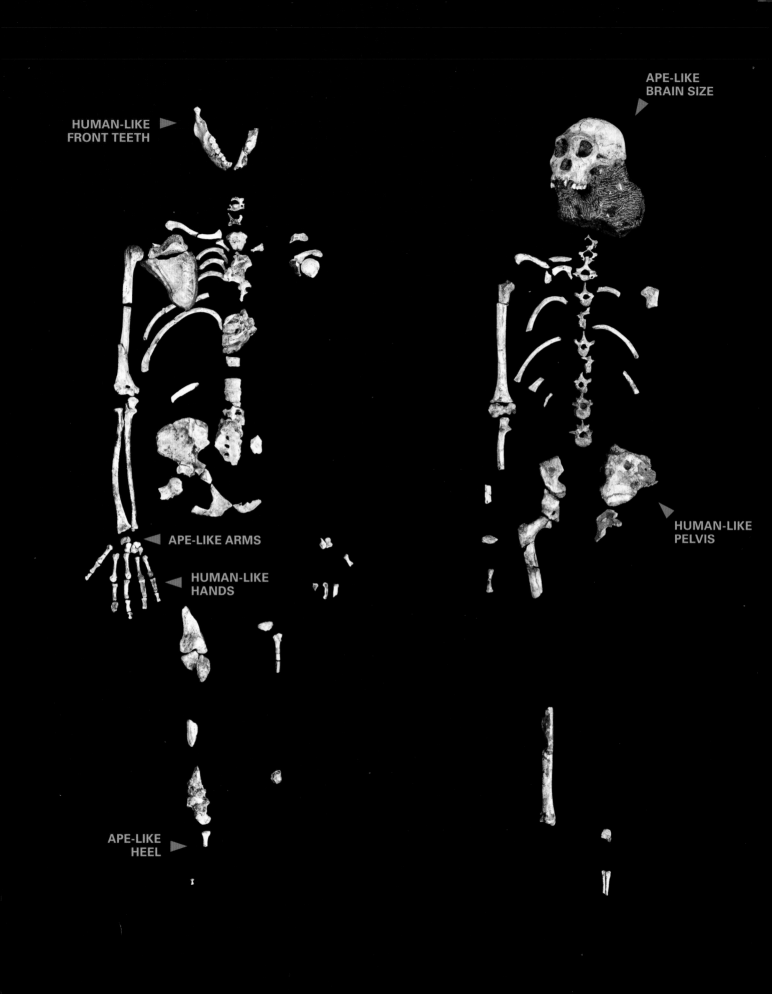

HUMAN-LIKE
FRONT TEETH

APE-LIKE
BRAIN SIZE

APE-LIKE ARMS

HUMAN-LIKE
HANDS

HUMAN-LIKE
PELVIS

APE-LIKE
HEEL

## CHAPTER SEVEN
# THE ANSWER

**When Lee turned over the stone** block, he noticed a jawbone with a tooth. Back in the lab, they found even more— the upper limbs of a partial skeleton. He could not wait to get back to the site, but he needed permission from the government to actually dig. Finally, on September 4, Lee and 13 colleagues returned to Malapa to examine the ancient cave.

The team arrived very early in the morning and in high spirits. One after another they tried to figure out where Matthew's block came from and thus where there might be more fossils. But as they broke for tea at 10:00 a.m., they had nothing to show for their labors. Could it be that the stone had been blasted out of one of the other 46 nearby caves—one destroyed by the miners? The sun was rising, clearing the shadows from one wall of the newly excavated pit. Lee spotted a bone—it was a humerus, yes, one of the same bones he had studied for his Ph.D.; then he saw a second, a scapula—another of the bones he had studied. He couldn't believe his luck! He stepped down into the pit, and as he placed his hand on the wall, two teeth fell into his hand. Lee was falling down the rabbit hole to Wonderland.

Matthew's find, it would turn out, was a bone from a young male, somewhere between 11 and 13 years old. We can estimate his age because we have since uncovered very nearly his entire skeleton. We can see where his bones were still growing and his teeth were erupting. But we will soon do better than that. In

Karabo, with the rock still attached to his skull, is on the right, and the adult female is on the left (OPPOSITE). Notice the mixture of features that make sediba such an intriguing anomaly.

France, one of the most expensive pieces of equipment in the world—a synchrotron—is analyzing his teeth. By counting the microscopic layers of enamel that grew when he was alive, it will give us his exact age in days.

A nationwide contest held to give the boy a name was won by Omphemetse Keepile, a girl who suggested Karabo, "the Answer." Karabo was about 1.3 meters, or 4.3 feet, tall and weighed somewhere between 30 and 45 kilograms, or 66 and 100 pounds (weight is harder to estimate than height, since all of his fat and muscle are gone). Because he was still growing, he would eventually have been taller than a second hominin Lee found at Malapa.

The synchrotron facility in Grenoble at night glows as if it were a grounded UFO.

Karabo's teeth and jaw about to be examined in the synchrotron

The second skeleton is an adult female. Could they be related, even mother and child? There is a remote possibility that we will be able to recover DNA—but we cannot wait for that slim chance. So experts are trying to invent new ways of determining how closely related two skeletons may be. Scientists have never had this problem before because no two such complete ancient hominin skeletons had ever been located right next to one another. It now seems very likely that fossilized skin can be made out next to the surface of some fragments from both skeletons—we have never even been close to recovering that before. And these are just a few of the vistas Malapa opens up for us.

Think of how unlikely this is. Before Matthew found Karabo, outside of Lucy, we had almost no nearly complete fossil hominin skeletons that could be dated to before 1.8 million years, and none from the crucial crossing period around two million years ago, a time between Lucy and our immediate ancestor *Homo erectus*. Lee himself had spent 17 years and found just a few fossil fragments—which is more than most experts find in their whole lives. Now we have two marvelous skeletons to examine, and soon we will have more. Lee and his team have found treasure beyond anyone's wildest pirate dreams.

We now know that there are fragments of at least four other hominins at Malapa. Determining when they were alive is another kind of detective story, but we have clever scientific tools to help us. We have learned how to read the secrets of the rocks that surround the sediba fossils.

A close-up of the child's femur minutes after it was discovered. The South Africa 2 Rand coin was put in the picture to add scale—it's about the size of a U.S. nickel.

## CHAPTER EIGHT

# DATING KARABO

**Why are the fossil bones** of our ancestors so rare, and so important? Starting from the time when Karabo was alive, all of the forces of nature work against us. Anyone killed by an animal would have had his or her skeleton pulled apart and gnawed. Even if a person died in a safe spot, there is every chance that the following endless centuries of wind, rain, rock slide, flash flood—as well as human construction or destruction—would have destroyed the remains. It is only by great fortune that any bones survive as fossils. That is, the skeleton is encased in soil, and over time, minerals replace the bone, preserving the exact shape of the original. So scientists have to go to places like dry river beds and ancient caves where fossils may have survived. They have to read back through the soil like a detective in a novel to figure out what kind of land formation, sealed by luck and time, might hold a secret.

If we start from the present, there are a new set of challenges. A fossil bone does not come with a tag—the scientist needs to determine how old it is and what it is. Neither of these questions is easy to answer. Archaeologists who study the history of human civilizations are lucky. Anything that was once alive has the element carbon in it, which we can use to figure out how old it is. But that method is only useful within about a 40,000-year span. Lucy, for example, was born over three million years ago. For fossils that old, carbon dating is useless to us.

We have recovered so many of Karabo's bones, and they are so well preserved, that this reconstruction (OPPOSITE) is probably accurate in almost every detail except for the nostrils—which cannot be precisely reconstructed from bones. Notice the slight smile (SEE PAGE 52).

The most obvious way to date a fossil is by using knowledge of the land: lower seems to mean older, since over time, one new layer of rock, or soil, or plants piles on top of another. But, as anyone who has ever dug at the seashore knows, a sudden slide can tilt that layer cake—and that is not to speak of earthquakes, cave-ins, or even the disturbances caused by burrowing animals

or spreading roots. Even if a bright scientist can line up the order of soil deposits and figure out which one originally held the fossil, that gives us a sequence, not a date. To work that out, scientists need a new set of clues.

One way to date something you find in the earth is by looking at what is near it. If a fossil is

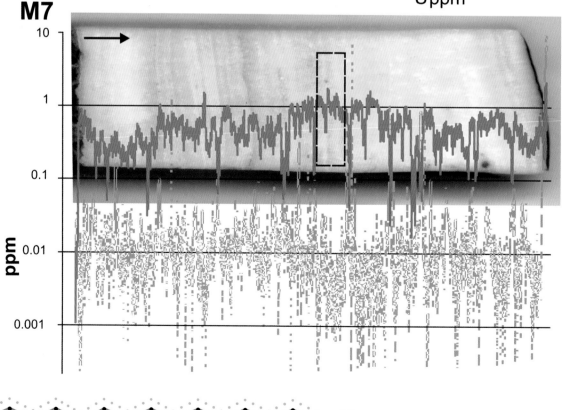

→ way up

$= =$ Pb total ppm

$^{238}$U ppm

M7

surrounded by the remains of ancient plants or animals, you research to find when they were alive. This kind of comparing and estimating is called relative dating—because it yields a general range of dates but not specific years. To get one step more precise—what scientists call absolute dating—you have to use what we have learned about the inner life of rocks.

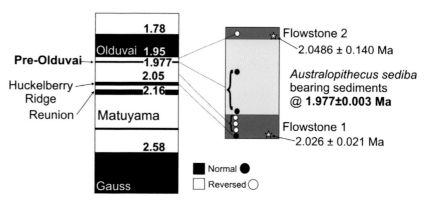

Since the 1960s, we have developed more and more clever ways to read the stories told by the radioactive elements trapped in stones. For example, if a rock formation contains lead, we are lucky because we know a lot about how lead is formed. Lead comes in four types or isotopes, and two of these are created over millions of years as the element uranium slowly decays. Measuring how much uranium is left and how much lead we have now tells us the age of the rock (uranium-lead dating). We have learned that the Earth's magnetic poles periodically reverse—what is now north was south. If there are iron particles in the soil, we can measure which way they are oriented (toward current or earlier magnetic poles)—and compare that to a carefully mapped time line of magnetic reversals—like matching up lines on a bar code (paleomagnetic dating). By greatest fortune, the sediba fossils rest between two layers of stone, which allows us to use both the uranium-lead and paleomagnetic dating methods. The orientation of small particles similar to iron filings fit one particular reversal of the Earth's magnetic poles that took place between 1.977 and 1.98 million years ago—a tiny 3,000-year window. We know exactly when sediba lived, but what kind of creature was it? More human? More ape-like? How can we tell?

We are back to comparison, only this time the game is more complex. We know a great deal about modern humans and about

The sediba fossils were found sandwiched between two layers of flowstone dated by the uranium-lead method. The magnetic particles near the fossils were then matched to the magnetic pole reversal that took place between 1.97 and 1.98 million years ago. As a result, we know exactly when sediba was alive.

our closest living relatives, modern chimpanzees. But what happens when you find a bone that has human-like qualities— for example, a body built to walk on two feet or a hand with an opposable thumb—and chimp-like qualities—for example, a small brain or conical-shaped chest? And what if many of these bones are fragmented, distorted, or broken? The scientist is faced with the most taxing jigsaw puzzle. He or she has to look at every other similar fragmentary fossil and try to line them up into a story of before and after. At one time scientists assumed they could arrange the bones in a clear ladder: chimp, chimpish animal that walked upright, walking on two legs with larger brain, human. But so many different and puzzling branches of ancestors have been found that no one can say for sure which led to what.

We now believe that nature tried all sorts of experiments in the millions of years during which troops of animals that walked upright on two feet lived in Africa. Making sense of this wide variety of bones has churned up so many more questions than answers that even the terms are changing. We used to speak of "hominids"—the large group including us, our ancestors, and our primate relatives. Now Lee, and many other scientists, prefer to say "hominins"—meaning only humans and our human-like relatives—treating this cluster as distinct from the chimpanzee, gorilla, bonobo, orangutan, and gibbon group. But if experts argue over how to lump or split clear human and clear nonhuman, think of how difficult it is to map out what once lay between us.

Matthew's find adds one huge new piece to the puzzle.

# Time line: Famous Fossil Finds from Africa

**1924** Raymond Dart discovers the Taung Child at Buxton, South Africa, and names a new genus and species, *Australopithecus africanus*—meaning "southern Ape of Africa." He estimates its age at over a million years. It would later be shown to be around 2.5 million years old.

**1947** Robert Broom and John Robinson find the most complete cranium yet discovered of an early human at Sterkfontein Cave in South Africa. Newspapers dub the cranium "Mrs. Ples"—a nickname for the genus and species Broom placed it in, *Plesianthropus transvaalensis*. It would later be put into the same genus and species as the Taung Child.

**1959** Louis and Mary Leakey discover at Olduvai Gorge in Tanzania a giant toothed species of early human the press would nickname "nutcracker man," which was easier than its scientific name, *Zinjanthropus boisei*! Just a few years later, in 1962, they would discover a bigger brained hominin, in association with tools, that would be called *Homo habilis*, meaning "Handy Man."

**1974** Donald Johanson and Tom Gray discover not only the most complete early hominin skeleton ever found, but the oldest, at Hadar, in Ethiopia. At more than three million years old, "Lucy," a member of a new species called *Australopithecus afarensis*, became a superstar of the fossil world almost overnight.

**1984** On the west side of Lake Turkana, in northern Kenya, Kamoya Kimeu, part of Richard Leakey's hominin gang, discovers the skeleton of a young boy that would be nicknamed "Turkana Boy." A member of the species *Homo erectus* and dating to about 1.6 million years, the strapping youth, as he was sometimes called, actually turned out to have a slightly deformed spine.

**1992** A team in Ethiopia led by Tim White finds the first remains of what is argued at the time to be the oldest hominin yet discovered, between 4.5 and 5 million years. They name the new genus and species *Ardipithecus ramidus*.

**1996** Under the direction of Ron Clarke, Stephen Motsumi and Nkwane Molefe discover deep underground at Sterkfontein Cave a remarkably complete skeleton of what might turn out to be a new species of hominin. Dubbed "Little Foot," the skeleton was at the time the most complete yet discovered and dates to around 2.5 million years old.

**2001** A team led by Michel Brunet discovers possibly the oldest hominin in Chad, *Sahelanthropus tchadensis*. At between six and seven million years old, "Toumai," as the find is nicknamed, is very close to the time of the split between chimpanzees and the hominin lineage.

**2008** Matthew and Lee Berger discover the first pieces of *Australopithecus sediba* at Malapa.

1 ◄

2 ►

▼ 3

## SEEING INSIDE THE
## SKULL. Lee carried the Malapa skull to the
synchrotron in Grenoble, France, in order for it
to be examined by ultrapowerful X-rays. **1** Lee
examines the specimen for damage. The skull
was shipped in a shockproof case, but he still
needed to check. **2** The skull was then placed
into a specially made container and locked in
place in front of the beam. **3** The beam is so
powerful Lee had to watch through a small lead-
lined safety window. **4** Lee and his colleagues
eagerly watched as the images came in live from
the synchrotron. **5** Finally, the complete image
was assembled, the highest resolution digital
reproduction of a fossil hominin skull in history.

5 ►

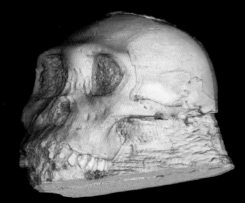

4 ▲

## CHAPTER NINE

# THE SOURCE

**How did Karabo and five others** die in the cave at Malapa? Lee named the discovery *Australopithecus sediba*. Sediba is a kind of pun. It means wellspring—because, very likely, millions of years ago the cave was a sort of natural well. The hominins probably fell into it searching for water. The boy's arms are fractured just where they would be if he had been trying to break his fall. The chemistry of the wet soil was such that as the bodies decayed, the mud quickly hardened into a kind of concrete— guarding the bones as they turned into fossils. But another word for wellspring is "source"—of water, yes, but perhaps in another sense, of us, of human beings.

What is sediba, and what can it tell us?

Primates travel in groups, like the baboons that greet visitors to the Cradle—as indeed we tend to live in families. Most probably Karabo was with his relatives, making his way through stands of large yellowwood trees, in a dangerous and dry world. Malapa holds the bones of saber-toothed cats and hyenas—carnivores who may also have fallen while desperate for water. As we know from the Taung Child, killers could swoop down from the skies. Yet sediba had immensely valuable traits that separated it from chimpanzees.

Sediba's hand is hauntingly similar to that of modern humans—with a fully opposable thumb. A chimpanzee's hand is excellent for grasping and swinging from trees. Sediba's hand

Lee worked carefully with the artist John Gurche to envision Karabo's fatal fall (OPPOSITE).

could hold and use small objects. Sediba's head is tiny, and it held a brain that is just on the edge of the chimpanzee range in size. But sediba's brain is organized differently from that of a chimpanzee, and the areas that are bigger might have to do with language and more complex problem solving. Surely, Karabo's group made sounds—not words or sentences, but perhaps calls—or even hand gestures that served as a form of sign language. And finally, sediba had odd feet—while his heel is quite different than ours, he probably did not have a grasping toe like an ape. His body was adapted to function in trees but also to walk on two feet on the ground.

The picture sediba paints is one of mixture. Sediba had the long arms of an ape, with a hand more human-like than other hominins, even some from later dates. It had that tiny brain, but the relatively small difference in size between Karabo and the adult female seems similar to humans, as is his rather small canine teeth. He was not built to terrify other males. Indeed the structure of the bones near his mouth suggests that—unlike chimpanzees—he could smile. When Lee describes all of these intriguing and puzzling traits you hear something different in his voice. Sure he is a scientist, and he is an able public speaker who has outlined all this many times, to everyone from Nelson Mandela to Jane Goodall to Bill Clinton. But there is a tenderness in his words, something that even sounds like love. He loves this strange creature his son found in the rock, this gift from ancient times given to him by the gopher tortoise, the eagle hunters, and Google Earth. He loves it perhaps most of all because sediba itself is—well—an anomaly.

Karabo's teeth are so well preserved we were able to get a very good picture of his diet. Almost all primates eat whatever is around them. Indeed one line of hominins is known for its large teeth—designed to crush anything from meat to tough plants. Karabo ate a different diet, perhaps focused on berries, seeds,

Karabo's fossil fingers cupped inside a modern hand. This strange being from nearly two million years ago had fingers hauntingly similar to ours.

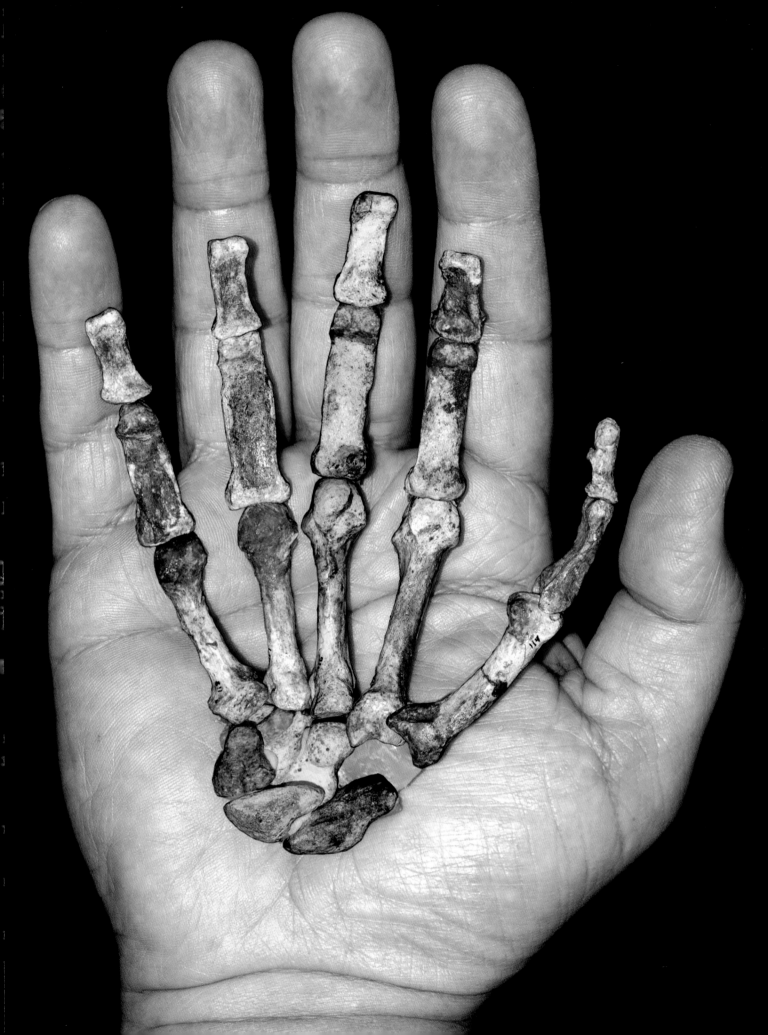

fruit, and maybe even bark. Only a few other distant relatives of ours, such as the Savanna chimpanzee, are such picky eaters. Anthropologist Jill Pruetz argues that these particular chimps make spears and show other remarkably human traits. Could it be that sediba also knew how to make tools? Lee Berger the scientist

Studies of sediba's teeth suggest it may have eaten similar foods to the diet we can trace when we examine the teeth of Savanna chimps.

says it is way too early to make that claim. But when you look in his eyes you see a gleam, and you know he is trying out that speculation in his ever active and lively mind.

The more we examine sediba the more we realize how little we know—and how much there is to learn. As William Kimbel, a paleoanthropologist at Arizona State University, told National Geographic, before sediba there were "only a handful of specimens from that time period. You could put them all into a small shoe box and still have room for a good pair of shoes." Sediba has exiled the shoes and demanded a bigger box.

That is what makes the discovery so exciting—it will now be up to the next generations of explorers—perhaps including people who are inspired by this book as Lee was by *Lucy*, to fill in those blanks. And, as we explain on page 59, Lee will help.

First, we have to think about how to search. Lee digs things out of the earth and, indeed, Matthew's clavicle was blasted into his path by the miner's dynamite. Yet Lee is intensely aware of the danger of destroying evidence, or trampling nature. His wife Jackie is a trained radiologist, and her skill with a CT scanner allows scientists to see, and make models of, fossils while they are still encased in loose rock. Someday, Lee believes, we will not have to dig at all—we will see into the earth without cutting it open. Even his teenaged daughter Megan is developing new, prizewinning ways to determine how fast fossils would form at a site like Malapa. We will know more by understanding better how to look.

There is a second way that we have to see with new eyes. Unlike other books on human origins, this one does not have a chart showing which led to what, with handy dotted lines spelling out the links. There are many of those on the Internet, for example, at http://humanorigins.si.edu/evidence/human-evolution-timeline-interactive. But, as you will notice on page 60, Lee wants us to change the image we have in our minds: not a ladder leading up, or even a tree with branches, but a braided stream where different species interbred in ways we are only starting to understand.

That image of connection, peoples flowing together, happens to also be featured on the flag of South Africa. Which brings me to one last meaning of sediba, the source. South Africa is a very new nation—it only finally freed itself of the chokehold of white rule in 1994. Everywhere you go in and around Lee's lab you feel the South Africans' sense of pride and ownership. This link to our ancient past is also a symbol of their new beginning.

As a South African government website explains, the Y shape at the heart of the country's flag can be seen as the coming together of diverse strands in South African society "taking the road ahead in unity."

## CHAPTER TEN
# WHAT IF LEE IS ALL WRONG ABOUT SEDIBA?

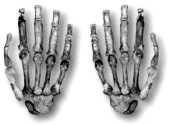

**I wrote this book** after reading about Lee, meeting him, and exploring Malapa with him as my guide. Clearly, it is his version of his past, his discoveries and their meaning. In general, the scientific community has embraced not only sediba but also Lee's approach to studying it. Still, as is usual in science, there are those who express doubt or hesitation about what sediba means—where it fits in the story of human evolution. And there are scholars who are equally excited about their own discoveries. Dr. Clarke, who cowrote the Taung Child paper with Lee, has spent more than 15 years working on the fossil called Little Foot. He believes it is the ancestor of those big-toothed hominins.

Lee's answer to those critics—and the point of view I take in this book—relates to something else I observed about him in his lab. Lee is a big spirit—a risk taker whose personality fits the Indiana Jones–style hat he sometimes wears. But he also likes collaboration, the hubbub of a group of peers. That suits science as it is now being practiced all over the planet—where younger experts value collaboration more than, or at least as much as, individual glory.

From the moment when Lee saw the bone in Matthew's hands, Lee's policy has been to share everything with the scientific community. Now that more than 85 scientists are working on aspects of sediba and Malapa, the game is out of Lee's

Lee in fine form, presenting his findings during a National Geographic lecture series in 2011 (OPPOSITE).

hands. The question is not whether he is right, but what the very best experts sharing ideas, competing in their interpretations, developing new techniques of inquiry, come to decide.

Sure sediba has been good to Lee—who is whisked off to all corners of the world to talk about it. But in a way it is no longer "his" discovery. He has handed sediba off to everyone—to you. For, just as he was sure, after finding the proof of the Taung Child eagle theory, that there were so many other clues all around him, he knows you will see what is invisible to him. And so in this book he is passing the baton—encouraging you to train your eyes, to walk the land, to learn to see the anomaly—to make the next key discovery. And because he knows that sediba is in the safe hands of the scientific community, and that you too will begin your own

Lee in his Indiana Jones hat out on a dig (TOP LEFT). Sediba made the cover of many magazines, including *Scientific American* (ABOVE).

searching, he is now free. Lee Rogers Berger can go back to doing what he loves: exploring.

To make sure that everyone who reads this book can take part in the adventure of science and discovery that began with Matthew and the clavicle, Lee and I have agreed to try an experiment. Every time a scientist finishes working on some aspect of sediba and announces his or her results to fellow experts in a research paper, we will explain those results to you at this site: www.scimania.org. Anyone who can read this book will know exactly as much about the frontiers of science, about the doors opened into human evolution by sediba, as the most senior, professional scientist. We have agreed to do this so that you can join in the hunt, so you can see what we miss, so that you are the ones to find the next beautiful anomaly.

One of the great mysteries of science is what became of the bones of "Peking Man," a fossil from around 500,000 years ago that was lost during World War II. Lee thinks he has the answer, and is visiting China to confirm it.

# THE BRAIDED STREAM: A NEW VIEW OF EVOLUTION FROM SEDIBA TO MODERN HUMAN

HOMO SAPIENS

HOMO FLORESIENSIS

HOMO NEANDERTHALENSIS

HOMO ERECTUS

HOMO HABILIS

HOMO GEORGICUS

HOMO RUDOLFENSIS

AUSTRALOPITHECUS SEDIBA

**MODERN GENETICS** and an ever-improving fossil record are altering scientists' views of how evolution works. While human evolution is often portrayed as a tree with many branches, Lee proposes that it may be better to use the image of a braided stream, with many different channels, some departing from the main stream to end in extinction, but with others rejoining, adding a bit back to the main flow. For example, we now know that Neanderthals interbred with modern humans and added small amounts of their genetic material to ours. In this braided stream image, we see a variety of species as nodes along the way from sediba two million years ago to the modern human.

# SUGGESTIONS FOR FURTHER READING

Since this is the first book—for any age reader—to describe sediba, all older books necessarily present views of human evolution that scientists are currently reexamining. Nevertheless, many of those books are thoughtful, clear, and based on careful research. That is not a contradiction because the essence of science is constantly to ask new questions, apply new methods, and make new discoveries. Here we select some excellent resources and divide them into the general background of human evolution—which is still useful—Lee's story, and sediba itself. This is like reading a popular series—you can only enjoy the later books if you have read the earlier ones—even if the story changes as it moves along.

## BACKGROUND

*Johanson, Donald, and Maitland Edey. *Lucy: The Beginning of Humankind*. Simon & Schuster, 1981.

Loxton, Daniel. *Evolution: How We and All Living Things Came to Be*. Kids Can Press, 2010.

Rubalcaba, Jill, and Peter Robertshaw. *Every Bone Tells A Story: Hominin Discoveries, Deductions, and Debates*. Charlesbridge, 2010.

Sloan, Chris. *The Human Story, Our Evolution from Prehistoric Ancestors to Today*. National Geographic, 2004.

*Tattersall, Ian. *The World from Beginnings to 4000 BCE*. Oxford University Press, 2008.

Thimmesh, Catherine. *Lucy Long Ago: Uncovering the Mystery of Where We Come From*. Houghton Mifflin, 2009.

Walker, Sally. *Written in Bone: Buried Lives of Jamestown and Colonial Maryland*. Carolrhoda, 2009.

## BOOKS AND ARTICLES RELATED TO LEE'S EARLIER WORK

Berger, Lee. "The Dawn of Humans, Redrawing Our Family Tree?" *National Geographic*, August 1998.

Berger, Lee with Brett Hilton-Barber. *In the Footsteps of Eve: The Mystery of Human Origins*. National Geographic Society, Adventure Press, 2000.

## SEDIBA

Fischman, Josh. "Part Ape, Part Human: A New Ancestor Emerges from the Richest Collection of Fossil Skeletons Ever Found." *National Geographic*, August 2011.

*Science*, September 9, 2011. Special feature on *Australopithecus sediba*.

Wong, Kate. "First of Our Kind: Could *Australopithecus sediba* Be Our Long Lost Ancestor?" *Scientific American*, April 2012.

## ONLINE RESOURCES ABOUT LEE

Lee's home page, with many resources on sediba and other projects
http://www.profleeberger.com/

Lee Berger, Paleoanthropologist and Explorer
http://www.nationalgeographic.com/explorers/bios/lee-berger/.

National Geographic Live!: Part Ape, Part Human: The Fossils of Malapa, November 21, 2011
http://www.youtube.com/watch?v=FFuwyBEq1IA.

NPR. Transcript and audio recording of Dr. Berger's interview, Examining Ancient Fossils for Clues to Human Origins, September 9, 2011
http://www.npr.org/2011/09/09/140337459/examining-ancient-fossils-for-clues-to-human-origins.

Website for updates on sediba, written for readers of this book
www.scimania.org.

## ONLINE RESOURCES ABOUT HUMAN ORIGINS

Human Origins, American Museum of Natural History
http://www.amnh.org/education/resources/exhibitions/humanorigins

*Understanding Evolution, a rich resource on evolution, developed by a team at University of California, Berkeley
http://evolution.berkeley.edu/evolibrary/article/evo_01

What Does It Mean to Be Human? Smithsonian National Museum of Natural History
http://humanorigins.si.edu

*Aimed at teachers, parents, and high school–aged readers.

# ENCYCLOPEDIA OF HUMAN ORIGINS
## (A GLOSSARY/INDEX)

**Karabo:** The popular name given to the sediba child's skeleton by Omphemetse Keepile, who won a nationwide contest in South Africa. *See pages 37, 38, 40, 43, 51, 52, and 63.*

**Job Kibii:** A postdoctoral student in Lee's lab in 2008 and now a research scientist at Wits. Kibii was with Lee and Matthew when Matthew discovered Karabo's clavicle. *See pages 35 and 40.*

**Little Foot:** A very complete skeleton of an as yet unnamed species of hominin from Sterkfontein dated to about 2.5 million years. *See* Ron Clarke *(opposite),* Sterkfontein Caves *(this page), and also pages 31, 47, and 57.*

**Lucy:** The 3.2 million-year-old hominin skeleton discovered by the American paleoanthropologist Donald Johanson in Ethiopa in 1974. Johanson later wrote a bestselling book about his discovery, which he also called *Lucy.* Lucy is considered an example of the hominin species *Australopithecus afarensis. See pages 17, 18, 40, 43, 47, 54, 57, and 61.*

**Malapa:** A tree-shaded cave near Gladysvale where Matthew Berger found Karabo's clavicle. Lee later decided to call this place Malapa, which means "homestead" in Sesotho. *See pages 21, 32, 33, 34, 35, 37, 38, 39, 40, 41, 44, 47, 48, 51, 55, 57, 61, 62, and 64.*

**Opposable thumb:** A thumb that can move across or opposite to the other fingers of the hand, useful for grasping objects and a characteristic of modern humans and some of our hominin ancestors. *See pages 46 and 51.*

**Paleoanthropologist:** A person who studies ancient humans and their behavior. *See pages 17, 54, 61, and 63.*

**Paleomagnetic dating:** We know precisely when the Earth's magnetic poles have reversed so we can match tiny magnetic particles with a chart, and thus determine the age of the surrounding rock. *See page 45.*

**Republic of South Africa:** The modern nation of South Africa. *See pages 7, 10, 15, 23, 24, 27, 28, 32, 41, 47, 55, 62, 63, and 64.*

**Saber-toothed cats:** These extinct members of the carnivorous cat family were fearsome predators and probably hunted our ancestors. *See page 51.*

**Savanna chimpanzee:** Some scientists believe these woodland animals who live in Senegal and Mali make spears and show other human-like behaviors. *See page 54.*

**Scapula:** The shoulder blade. *See page 37.*

**Sterkfontein Caves:** One of the richest hominin sites in the world, located in the Cradle of Humankind. The skeleton of Little Foot was found here as well as important fossils like Mrs. Ples. *See* Ron Clarke *(opposite),* Little Foot *(this page), and also pages 31, 32, and 47.*

**Synchrotron:** A circular particle accelerator that generates X-rays that can be used in various scientific experiments. *See pages 38, 39, 48, and 49.*

**Taung and Taung Child:** The Taung Child is a hominin fossil identified by Raymond Dart in 1924. The skull is thought to be 2–3 million years old and was the first member of the hominin species *Australopithecus africanus* to be identified. *See pages 23, 24, 25, 28, 29, 47, 51, 57, 58, and 62.*

**Uranium-lead dating:** The use of the decay of radioactive uranium to inert lead to date fossil-bearing rock or flowstones. *See pages 44 and 45.*

**Vervet monkeys:** A medium-size monkey whose body coloring is often silvery gray or greenish-olive. *See page 23.*

**Wildcatter:** A person who drills oil wells on his own, often in areas where there is high risk and no sure success. *See pages 13 and 14.*

**World Heritage Site:** A place that is listed by UNESCO, a division of the United Nations, as being of special cultural or natural importance to all humanity. *See pages 7 and 62.*

# MY PART IN THIS BOOK
## BY MARC ARONSON

**Lee Berger** wanted to write a book for young readers because when he was growing up he had the terrible feeling that all the big discoveries had already been made. In fact, as sediba shows, they are just starting to take place. As it happens I said exactly the same thing in *If Stones Could Speak*, and so Jennifer Emmett of National Geographic matched us up. I just wanted to be sure that I could go to South Africa to see Lee and visit Malapa, and I hoped my son Sasha could interview his son Matthew. National Geographic agreed, and the adventure began.

To prepare for my trip I quickly read Ian Tattersall's *The World from Beginnings to 4000 BCE*. It is much easier to talk with an expert when you know the terms he or she will use and the main debates and controversies in the field. I strongly urge any student working on a report to do your background reading before emailing an author or professor—they will never write your report for you, but they can add delicious insights.

As I have tried to show in this book, Lee is a dynamic, larger-than-life figure. You almost see the many ideas, plans, and theories he is juggling as you speak with him. But he is also relaxed, at ease, ready to share a joke. My challenge was to understand the science, capture his personality, and, most of all, pass along the vision that brought both of us this project: You, the person reading these lines, can make amazing discoveries. They are out there, waiting for you. Once you study what is known and begin to ask new questions, you will begin to see the anomalies. I hope that message comes through on every page.

By filming Lee as they walked through the Cradle, Marc captured a visual record of Lee's story.

Sasha exploring Malapa. He later Skyped in to his science class in the U.S. to share the experience.